Mistaking the Sea for Green Fields

Akron Series in Poetry

Mistaking the Sea for Green Fields

Ashley Capps

The University of Akron Press
Akron, Ohio

All inquiries and permission requests should be addressed to the Publisher,
The University of Akron Press, Akron, Ohio 44325-1703.

ACKNOWLEDGMENTS

Thanks to the editors of the following publications in which these poems first appeared: *American Poetry Review:* "Black Ice," "Encore," "Inside Facts"; *The Iowa Review:* "Poem on the Occasion of My MRI," "Hymn for Two Choirs,"; *Margie: The American Journal of Poetry:* "God Bless Our Crop-Dusted Wedding Cake"; *Post Road:* "Reading an Ex-Lover's First Novel," "Hwy 51."

"I Used to See Her in the Field beside My House" appeared in the anthology *And We the Creatures* (Dream Horse Press, 2003), edited by C. J. Sage.

I am indebted to the Wisconsin Institute for Creative Writing and the Iowa Arts Council for generous fellowships that provided invaluable time toward the writing of this book. Thanks to my teachers and patient readers over the years: Erin Belieu, Mark Wunderlich, Jim Galvin, Dean Young, Tracey Knapp, Melissa Tuckey, Josh Bell, and Nam Le. My deepest gratitude to Cathy Smith Bowers—nothing was possible without you. Thanks, most of all, to my family—fiercely; boundless love.

LIBRARY OF CONGRESS CATALOGING-IN-PUBLICATION DATA
Capps, Ashley, 1976–
  Mistaking the sea for green fields / Ashley Capps. — 1st ed.
    p. cm. — (Akron series in poetry)
  ISBN-13: 978-1-931968-37-9 (pbk. : alk. paper)
  ISBN-10: 1-931968-37-3 (pbk. : alk. paper)
  I. Title.
  PS3603.A668M57 2006
  811'.6—DC22

                    2006024313

The paper used in this publication meets the minimum requirements of American National Standard for Information Sciences—Permanence of Paper for Printed Library Materials, ANSI Z39.48–1984.∞

Cover: "Man's Best Friend," mixed media on paper, Claudine Hellmuth, 2005.

Contents

Dad—

My ship, laden with forgetfulness, passes through a harsh sea, at midnight, in winter, between Scylla and Charybdis, and at the tiller sits my lord, rather my enemy.
—Petrarch

I

Hymn for Two Choirs

Best apple I ever had was three o'clock
in the morning, somewhere outside
San Francisco, beach camping, stars holding
the sky together like sutures. I was thinking
how I was going to get old and ask myself
why did I only live for one thing;
at the same time I didn't know how to change.
I thought I felt like my neighbor's huge dog—
every day stuffed into a small man's green T-shirt
and chained to a stake in a yard of incongruous
white tulips. Here and there a red bird, a train.
Way down the beach other tents glowed orange.
I heard a stranger call my name
and another stranger, laughing, answered.

God Bless Our Crop-Dusted Wedding Cake

When my mother lifted her shirt
to show the sunken grave of her breast,
the fresh tarantula tattoo she'd chosen

over reconstruction, I shuddered at first.
The last bad joke she'd play on her body—
chest half-spider, fanged, half-planetary:

lone red nipple circling like Jupiter's
perpetual storm—and I but spectator
to so much bad weather. Like summer

1967, when she roped me to the pier,
when I was ten and she was drunk in her bikini
and wanted to watch the hurricane come in.

The green sky spun like an automated car wash!
Acorn barnacles oatmealed my back. A population
of lobsters blew past like the rusty contents of a toolbox.

Dad took one look at my rope burns and punched her;
but Mom wore her bruises like high art, her broken
nose a study in cubism, blue flowers blooming

under her skin like watercolor.
But there were times we acted like a family.
Dad came home with a telescope, and we watched the stars

fall into the ocean like broken teeth.
We sipped Jim Beam from muscular teacups,
channeled my grandmother who finally showed up

in her bank-robber uniform, sweet smile pig-faced
through the stocking, but dear nonetheless.
Ours was the best-dressed scarecrow,

in Dad's bowling shirt and Mom's peekaboo
lace thong. The landscape was wrong for birds
but it kept Jehovah's Witnesses away. Which is

not to say we never prayed. When my mother knelt,
I could hear her rattlesnake rattler earrings
chatter like rosary beads in the darkness. She prayed

for my sister to take the For Sale sign off
of her body and come home to sleep in a new pair
of soft pajamas. My sister could not.

So while it is true she has cleared the atmosphere celestial, left me
gravity-strapped and mourning, blistered through cloud cover,

while she has gifted me one schizoid father's government-issue
ashes, one grey-eyed sister's prostitute bones, a brief family

history in cardboard, percussive teeth and my double helix permanently scarred;
while it is true she daily christened the oarless boat of my childhood,

she never broke a single bottle against me.
So if my mom shows up in her ghost bikini with both breasts intact and a lasso

chasing my neck through a sandstorm—I'll let her.
I'll hand her a beer and watch my huge flip-flops fly off in the wind.

Reading an Ex-Lover's First Novel

I don't mind if you say *her blouse*
fell open like thunder, or if you recall
the amethyst veins inside her eyelids, the sand
in the delicate ditch of her neck. Go ahead

and compare the strung lights of the pier
to white streamers behind a black wedding car.
And those sea oats, scraping
under the constellations, did console.

But I have a problem
with the way you describe the body
of the crab washed up that morning
as an orchid, as a music box, as

if it were intact, when in fact
the thing was pink chunks of meat
that floated away from each other,
blue broken pieces of shell on a gut string.

You saw it. You
were there—

that enormous claw, dangling
like a polite, ridiculous teacup.

April

Everywhere, the ghost
wigs of dandelions,
everywhere the green
toothache of early spring.
The cops-in-training
are beating their horses,
and they wave at me
from the fields. All the girls
show their shoulders now.
The future promises more
of the same. It is hard
to love people enough.

Inside Facts

I found out they'd been grinding chickens up behind my house.

Spent egg hens,
throwing them into the woodchipper live by the thousands,
cheaper than the slaughterhouse.

What do you think I did when I found that out.

You may touch me now, I am tame.

The roses had
seemed to me like torches,
till the wind came and blew them away.

There's no middle ground,
only things and the soul

at a vast unbridgeable distance from them,
which my friend JB once noted
before jumping—

         Stiffneck,
this is it, that lilac
floating along the black water—

The clouds were not lit, on either side.
I probably want what Moses wanted.

Ars Poetica

There is a thing
some men will ache to do
and break themselves
against their lives and women, trying.
Women, too, have lost
their grip, having endeavored
or accomplished it. The devil
threads his needle,
and the string's a river
fat with fish
that wanted other words for it.

Live Feed

When I got to the Gate   there was no Gate
People were coming and going   freely   Few

wore white   At a picnic table   Jesus Christ
sitting there with Adam Smith who said *Ask her*

They were playing a card game and Jesus motioned me over
You ask her he said   At which point Smith looked down

at his watch—*Shit! You let me forget again!*—
and pulled a flea circus out of his breast pocket

knocking the cards from Jesus's hand   who had
clearly been winning   all along   Smith slipped me a note

Jesus loves you do you love Him check Yes or No

When I looked back   Christ was lifting his robes   and Smith
hovered over a wound in his side   with a tiny dropper

The Zealot

Now that I no longer offer my thumb
to your car, my apologies
to your insulted face,

now that I've gotten the word out,
now that they're converting
in unanticipated numbers,

I have to drink beers every night
so I can still tell a joke.

They don't help my life.

What I do is pour cereal into the bowl
and forget there's no milk,
there is no milk at all—

and it would have been sufficient,

exactly enough
for a little while.

Black Ice

In the porcelain artist's painting, the mistress
languishes behind a screen.

> She receives her pain.

I sleep, eat, the egg slides over the pan,
the flyers say *WE ARE SLAVES TO THE CAPITALISTS*
or they say *CARPET STEAMED 4 LESS*;

> it's almost Christmas.

The light is gone by six o'clock.
I force narcissus in a bowl of shallow rocks.

On channel three, a teary Miss America is planting kisses
on the small bald heads at the children's cancer ward.

Across the street, my neighbor's yard blinks:

HAPPY! BIRTHDAY! BABY! JESUS!

> Love rises

like a blister on the season.

☆

Have I even set the stage right?

Bare interior.
Grey light.
Left/right back: two small windows, curtains drawn.

WINTER calls to SPRING:

> Are we still going apple-picking today?

SPRING (a long pause):

> I remember you. . . . I think I do.

Dear God of Detachedness, I am separate.

God of the Sea, I adore the tide, its long milk mustache full of sparks.

And the moon so like a salt lick—we were sick once,

                                   my sister and I;
all summer long we slept like tubers, back to back.
The long curtain blew in over the bed.

That house is gone now, all those lilacs,
and the bait shop where some kids beat a man to death
with rakes and shovels.

Someone's life was always an emergency,
someone's mother sobbing soaking her head in kerosene,
someone's sister losing it early down by the tracks.

And Ace died of steroids,
and Daddy came home from the chicken farm one night,
saying, *Nothing is funny.*

After years, my lover would not leave his wife.

☆

I drank enough wine to marry myself.
I was too drunk to carry me over the threshold;
punished the neighbor's roses instead,
but he forgave me.
In a photograph of my father, there's just a head
sticking out of the waves. The sun is white.

My mother always liked to say he was out to sea.
She liked to say that was what I inherited,
always being out to sea.
But you can tell it was shallow water.
I think he had lifted himself on his knees.

As Surprised by That as by Everything That Followed

The Days Inn accepted my dog, for example.

I pulled off the side of the road until I could see
to get to a motel.

The blizzard itself caught me unawares.

And where was I going
with such a rusted-out chassis,
my father wanted to know,
repositioning the Christmas tree
and noting it had been perhaps improper
curbside placement and he wasn't
the target of anything.

II

Hwy 51

for J

Already the clouds of white flies have risen
up into evening. My right hand's awake
and drums music into the wheel. On the soft lawns
the dogs jerk their chains. I guess they want
and want. A child pitched a fit
in the mall today and her father said
You are behaving horribly
into her hair and then he kissed her:
may your son's sleeplessness and his shrieks
and his little white fists be appeased in your arms
and may that become a kind of happiness
for you. Here, it's dusk. Big trucks grope the road
and carry the mystery somewhere else.

The Sign Said

THERE ARE SOME MESSES
NO ONE SHOULD HAVE
TO CLEAN UP   CALL US
YOUR HOMICIDES   SUICIDES ETC.
I thought about my own Etc.
also I thought about worst jobs
What's yours was one of my favorite questions
at parties   the last time I asked it
this girl I knew said Phone Sex
Operator   which was a thing she did
to get attention at parties   although it was true
the part about her having that job
but not the part about not liking it
you'd have thought I'd identify
with her loneliness and her need for attention
but I didn't   I subtly mocked her
which was a thing I did   and do   I didn't
appreciate the way she used her boobs
at the same time as making high literary references
or how she grinned and said *Tell them yours*
because I was a maid at a Motel Six
which was actually all right
but a maid before that for this country club bitch
who on my first day pointed to a pool
of fresh poodle vomit and said
You'll need to take care of that
and speaking of signs
the only reason I didn't quit right then
was an ant crawled out
of a pile of toenail clippings   lifting
the largest one like a sail

A *La Recherche Du Temps* . . . (Six Steps (For Example))

Spoke to the cockroach, saying:
                                    You little thug.

And thuglike, too, provoked
by thought
                    one yellow evening in October,

packed the truck

and picked the lock

and read, dismayed, the guest list (it
did not include me)

and woke up naked, without a costume,
except for the wings someone glued to my ass.

To the Dapple Critic

Try to explain to M. Renoir that a woman's torso is not a mass of
flesh in the process of decomposition with green and violet spots
which denote the state of complete putrefaction of a corpse!
—Albert Wolff, 1876, on Nude in the Sunlight

You must have never been inside the orchard—
never seen the leopard

way light lay on apples
through their leaves.

You must have never bargained
on your knees in any church,

then stood to find the prismed round
a rose window flung at your feet.

You must have never swum
beyond the tide, observed how pink

anemones swell beneath
transparent veils of kelp.

You must have tried all night
to just erase the obscene

landscape of her dappled skin;
and finally, to still one restless hand,

you leapt from bed and grabbed that
hateful pen.

You must have never loved her
more than then.

Mistaking the Sea for Green Fields

Ophelia, when she died,
lay in the water like the river's bride, all pale
and stark and beautiful against the somber rocks,
her hair an endless golden ceremony.
She made the water sing for her; it flowed
over her folded arms.

Not so my father's sister Karen,
swollen in a day-old tub of water
when they found her,
needle tucked into the fold of her arm,
her last thing: a wing.

So everything went as nameless as the men
who lifted her naked from the tub,
or those who rolled her
into the mouth of the furnace,
which is what you get
when you don't get a service,
when your mother's years of grief turn
last to rage: *I won't pay for it.*
Leave me out of this.

And even though they finally said
it wasn't suicide; a mistake—
no one knew what to do
with all of that anger,
or in the end how not to blame her.

Even now, in her unmarked container.

☆

People once believed a deeper reason, some dark secret
motivation to the way the lemmings threw themselves
en masse into the sea. Were they weary
of their lives; could they, too, despair?
Or like those second-vessel swine
when Jesus exorcised two babbling men of their demons,
driving the demons through a pack of bewildered hogs—
the way *they* plunged?

The truth we know now: they leave when food is scarce,
when they've grown too many;
believe the roads they follow
lead to new meadows, a place to start over.

I think of Karen, feeding
and feeding her veins, how it is possible
she saw us all suddenly there—miraculous
and festive on some bright and other shore,
like the life she had been swimming toward
all along, trying to get right.
Like those sailors long ago,
that tropical disease, *calenture*—
when, far from everything they knew,
men grew sometimes delirious
and mistook the waving sea for green fields.
Rejoicing, they leapt overboard,
and so were lost forever,
even though they thought it was real, though
they thought they were going home.

My People

We bury the sofa for no good reason
Who poisoned Jim's meds
Who pistol-whipped Stick's buddy's sister
Who lashed those   cumulonimbus
                            clouds to the highway, Lord?
We pray for our enemies
We pray for the elms and the poplars
We are some damn switch hitters
The sky, the sky, we always say
You can hear the knife slide through the sun

Home Stay

Comme un gypsy, she railed,
exactement comme un gypsy, and I understood

my mistake. I had hung my laundry
on the wrong side of the house,

out the window no less, ignorant
of the etiquette of drying, too poor

to pay for the machines. I'd been surviving
on baguettes and water for weeks,

as she resented my *vegetable ethics*,
and still made glazed duck for two every Sunday.

Lonely old woman. I bled on her bed
for hours one night. Woke horrified

to see how the hemorrhagic butterfly had spread
between my legs. My red

face as I tried to explain that *mes regles*
were not, in fact, regular. I dragged

the mattress out into the street, unprepared,
with my stupid tears, for the lecture

of lemon trees blooming in every front yard.
How perfectly yellow! How fragrant

the blouses flapping politely from balconies!
How wonderful to be a girl

lugging her stain through the public square,
where no one stared,

where people were falling in love left and right
as a result of the architecture.

Elegy for My Old Urgency

If it was before or after I bought the white halter,
I don't remember, but that summer I went platinum.
For ten bucks more, they rolled it and set me under
a dryer facing the street.

The heat hung thick as slugs, stuck to the red geranium petals. Panting,
squirrels flattened themselves like pelts.

O peroxide!
O chemical steam!

It seemed I had merely to think of a man, or glance
into the ornamental cabbages whimsically.
There were odes to my buttocks, movie tickets, neckties in my teeth.
I shaved my legs with a bowl of suds in a window seat, completely naked;

I would never be the baker's wife, with her spreading yellow teeth,
spotted hands flipping over the CLOSED sign, dragging
her shaggy parasol down the street.

December

Back from the morgue   the snow
a feeble blue   strung lights stutter
in the streets   shop windows breathe
with animated dolls   doll families 'round
the fire   the Tree   one mother's lost
her plastic hand   the stump of wires   gropes
the air   above her doll son's head
the hand   rests   on his yellow hair
how many violations   of the flesh?
how many ways   we never plan   we'll be
undressed   She   was drunk
she did not say   I would like   for this to happen
she said   NO   no   but one had her
by the hair   the other   peeling off her panties   so
she waved her arms   a symphony
till   it was over   my grandfather
believed   if he prepared   special red
sugar water   stood at the glass   as they sipped
the hummingbirds   finally   would let him enter
their hovering   they never did   they always
flew   Lord   when we were on our knees
so long   it was not gratitude   it was hunger

Gripes the Lover Leveled (Leaving)

Pronounced me: gaudy and ruthless.
I sewed the dog on the sweater,

yes, embellished the already
yellow umbrellas (took the Rust

Belt out of the girl; you *can*),
but you turned me into a fighter.

Found my offensive. Thanks
again for the thrust and parry,

the brass ring embrace,
the structural stress (in the leaves

and the waves oh), the thud
of my ass finally after

I couldn't keep up with it—
too much tough for even this

your lamé samurai, your grunt, your glass
plug-ugly agonist.

Bottleneck

He is the carpenter *and* the cook.
What is she?
She talks too much.
She points out individual clouds
on the river's surface. She walks
too slow. All the trees
stuck under the old train bridge
since last May's flood won't budge.
That shit aint going nowhere
without dynamite, he says, and spits. He knows
he talks like that. Rough, it is a way
of seeming reckless and indifferent.
It endears him to her, and she thinks
the river will fix itself.

The Wedding

The limousine breathes
on the side of the street

like a beached whale,
trailing tissue and condoms

like lampreys. Attempting

to stuff herself in, she flattens
her ruffles, presses down

her crinolines—
and, failing, falls

into his arms.
She is wide and white as a wave.

She will have to reduce
herself

substantially.

for Carla, 1949–1998

Otherwise

Of course there is a huge orange hot air balloon
floating somewhere without you.
That is as it should be.
You won't look up again in the driveway
and feel your heart deflate a little, turn
back to the groceries softening in their paper bags.

You won't wonder like that.

Your daughters were lovely.
Your geraniums blossomed wildly, kind of endless,
and your quiche lorraine made it hard to eat at home.
But he was no good for you, Carla,
the things that he made you do
and the way that he spoke to you—
how did you stay with him for so long
and how did you stay
so cheerful?
We liked how you always said
Hey, you when we pulled a prank,
and every time you answered the phone
and we said it was us.

Nobody could see.

The man at the wheel who sent you
flying to the trees, he couldn't see you
through his dreams, and through the darkness

of our closed eyes as we prayed
in the waiting room, we couldn't see God, not really,
and we couldn't see you, no matter how
we wept and raged in the doctors' faces.

You couldn't see anything, since you were sleeping.

You slept too deep, though, and the garden
of machines stood bright and useless.

You left us for good.

We don't plan on recovering, ever.
We don't plan on going back
to your peony garden to steal
the most beautiful plant by its roots.
It's somebody else's now,
and it's somebody else's house,
and of course there is a huge orange hot air balloon
leaving me behind.

It came so low a minute ago,
I thought it would land.
I thought, *Finally.*
Then it filled like a giant lung and flew away.

III

The Nearest Simile Is Respiration

To poetry

I was boozed I was doped I was maybe
a floozy before you knew me, loose
leafed like autumn and most of the books
of the Old Testament that fell out
of my father's Bible. I had a body.

I had a habit of hauling my telescope
into the outskirts, ransacking all
the toothsome blackness for what: a reason
not to do me in. Proof I was more
than the seasonal ragbag detritus
choking the rooftop gutters, more
than a piece of the cosmic dust
in some ruined philosophy.

I could not be consoled by the universal
Sisyphus in us all, the dung beetle
nuzzling its putrid globe.

I could not hitch my wagon. The stars
and stars abrade my notions of my Self;
tricuspid Eros chewed me raw; Jesus
Christ rubbed mud in my eyes, and I saw
not. I did not see.

But with you! my sweetheart hairshirt,
my syntactic gondolier, ruffian for hire, befoolable
irresolute Chanticleer: with you, I back-float
the massy and heretofore unnavigable childhood
algal blooms, where no fish swam. No fish
have swum that Mississippi.

With you, I forgive my father's notes
to NASA, the self-inflicted swastika tattoo,
my sister's coked-up juggernaut cannonball
into the afterlife.

I forgive the afterlife,
resurrect John Lennon and the jukebox
at the Quik 'N' Hot, infect myself
with a rare strain of tarantism. With you, I dance
the summum bonum. With you, I am greater
than or equal to the lack, and luck is weather
that permits my red begonias.

Public, Scenic

There is about to be a blizzard.
A helicopter is flying over.
A man is taking a woman's picture
in the gazebo,
saying, less prostitute, more
girlfriend-against-the-moonlight,
and she's saying, I'm not
against moonlight, I'm all for it,
and he's laughing hysterically
taking close-ups of her hair
which looks like a cloud
because of the snowflakes
sticking to it and everything else,
including the sign that says
this park is up for adoption
(in case you're interested);
but I wouldn't adopt this park—
no one picks up the dog poop
and everything's weird here,
even the rabbit in the snow
beneath the basketball goal,
looking at it like he's contemplating
a shot.

All Night City Train

Out the window   winter begins
to deliver   its luminous manifesto
The domes go by   The domes appear   and recede
green or gold   against the dark   and glow
like vegetables   I   had a spiritual inner life   On the side
of the dumpster   a foamy cocoon   dangling
from one pathetic fiber   I brought it inside
watched it for weeks   and felt
a kind   of nonglandular reverence   a mystical
realignment of Self   in the cosmic   echelon
But   the cocoon   was a used   cottonball
The shadow   breathing inside   was a stain
that belonged to someone   Nothing   was waiting
to be changed   into something   with wings

I Used to See Her in the Field beside My House

Perhaps it is the way your nipples,
long like fingers on an open hand,
beckon the tired, huddled, osteoporosis-fearing
masses to your swollen, steaming milk sack.

The skin of your huge behind ripples
where giant horseflies understand
only that you taste good, not that they hurt you while you're looking
out to pasture through a crack

in your stall. Cow, listen—forget the deep pools
of rain that pock the lit, green land-
scape of your youth. Forget the singing
man who rubbed your head. He's readying the rape rack.

In the end, you're skinned and processed. A hip pulls
loose, shoulders dismantle in the hands
of some masked worker. There is nothing
in this world that loves you back.

To My Friend Grievous

You—with your padlocked closet full
of popcorn buckets & monster trucks & the Fourth
of July & the last remaining truly whirling

                                        dervishes—

& your lassoed-in—I guess—ferris wheels, & your childhood
jack-in-the-boxes—I, too, have wept
the dissipated stars & the blanket
thrown over the firmament.

Or over the sun, whichever. Which shortly
stoppered my throat & left my laundry wet
on the line, & cold. I am old,
or I am young & old's fearful.

Cheers, then. Here's to the mold
sporulating invisibly beneath the bathtub, here's
to the all-circumscribing wane, & the seventeen-years-
in-the-making cicada sizzle:

dizzy with longing they open
their red eyes & Orpheus-like tunnel upwards,
& Orpheus-like they sing
for a lover, but are never torn apart.

Which is to say—
you are too attuned
to this darkness, too absorbent
of it, it

is like an enveloping velvet umbrella
above your soul—your *Self?* Your softer

chemicals, then, your You I
love, whatever *that* is—

We are human & alone, but someone
is playing a tambourine, yes, & a tuba
& I have vaguely heard the flame-eater's
tailpipe laughter. Bring back

the dancing bears, and I will improvise a spotlight.

Shane Says

Shane says he used to breed pit bulls back in the woods off his yard—
thirty dogs, thirty lengths of three-foot chain.

All they wanted to do was bite each other.

And there were plenty of people who wanted them that way.

One night, he heard a racket like the Gates of Hell.
Blue lights everywhere, knew he'd been found out.
He practiced saying, *A man's gotta make a living*
as he grabbed his gun and walked out back.
But the officers they were just laughing their asses off,
saying, *Buddy can you call off your dogs?*
We been chasing this fucker for over an hour,
and he made the mistake of running into your yard!

And there was a man lying on the ground
with each of his legs in a pit bull's mouth.
Shit, said Shane. *They don't let go—*
There's a special tool—so he got the tool,
straddled each of the dogs, cranked open the jaws—

Says, after, It looked like a couple of bowls of spaghetti
attached to a man.

What's the name of that tool, I ask.

Breakstick. Only thing that'll pry 'em off.

That so, I say, and the woods and the fields
and the roads disappear and it's quiet in the dark.

Tar

I knew   with a primal certitude   his blood
was becoming slow lava   chugging thick
Visualize your body   healing   I said
but he shook his head   and described
black luna moths   on his lungs
hungry flotillas   sourcing the lymph
and on his birthday   when we argued   over a cloud
resembling: a) a chandelier
b) a lesser-tentacled squid
c) (we both saw the lost photograph of my mother
unwinding   her pink foam curlers)   I knew
we had loved the same world
overwhelmed   by different ideas
about how it should be;
that the love faded naturally   with experience
but the ideas   died harder

Poem on the Occasion of My MRI

Fancy the brain from hell held out so long. Let go.
—John Berryman

Like a fat-headed fetus pushing feet-first through the mother;
like a half-eaten bug jutting up from the lips of a frog;
like Uncle Cross in Than Ke snaking into the enemy tunnel—

my body, my white legs protrude
from the tube
and it's tight and I ask
for a last-second sedative.

But nurse wants to know if I have a "driver."

—*Do you have a driver?*
(I do not have a driver.
Just as recently as last month I had a driver.
I *should* have a driver.)
—*I do not have a driver.*

I do not have a driver.

I'm floating
this particular river
in a boat for one.

Voice over the water:

The next scan will be three-and-a-half minutes. Hold completely still.

OK.

Sivabali Yogi sat twenty-three hours a day for eight years, his attention peacefully between his eyebrows.

I myself in eighth grade won a contest for least visible movement.

The prize was to be a human mannequin for Sears.

I kept my eyes on the swans in the pond in the middle of the mall.

☆

Always it begins behind the left eye: a tear, then throbbing.
Sometimes I speak to it as to a child: softly: *No,
not now. This isn't the time.* Yesterday

at Manzetti's, stuffing my mouth
with fresh bread, suddenly simply visionless—Marco Polo
in the pool and my first bikini, *Where are you?*

—*No, you have to say "Marco"
and we say "Polo!"*

Where are you?

Meaning, really, where am I
in relation to you?

Or to my wine, which I spilled, groping, ignoring the blackness.
The waiter looked ready to weep. *Your head was just lying there.
You wouldn't answer.* I've begun tipping over

midsentence. Twice at dinner with my parents.
Once near the end of a blow job. He didn't understand
what was happening. *Go home,* I stammered, *to your wife.*

Last week in front of my students, discussing "Dream Song #9."

It's golden here in the snow.

☆

This morning at the door, a representative
of The Mystic Truths of the Spirit World of
the Soul of All was scarfing down a doughnut.
He told me, *Go into the heart
of imagination with your eyes closed.
Then, you may see some beautiful light.*

Going into the mouth of the machine, I am trying.
My eyes are closed.
I have giant headphones playing a Beethoven CD.

It's supposed to distract my mind from being illogical
about the world of the senses.

☆

I learned to sleep with his arms and legs on me.
For once in my life, it did not feel too close.
Now the wide bed suffocates. The first week I cried
the kind of crying where you almost start to choke,
which happened frequently when I was a teenager.
Wonderbread my guinea pig did sympathy shakes.
I speak to her still because she sends me tiny messages
from the grave, full of grief. My father smacked her
with a shovel after I said go ahead, she was drowning
on her own fluids. Try as I may, I cannot
picture my spine as a tube of loving light. I cannot
find the peace glowing like a flame or moon
in the forehead and then the chest. *The next
scan will be fourteen minutes.* I speak into the emergency
microphone: *Please, set* Ode to Joy *at repeat.*

Washing the Brain

But first I must tie up the dogs.
I am washing my brain
because, while relatively small,
it has been much handled:
There was a cook who borrowed it
to flavor the chowder; it was better
than garlic or bones, and it sang
from the bottom of the pot. Thus,
they survived the shellfish shortage.

There followed a priest
who rubbed it like a lucky marble
between sermons; a sequined circus
performer who juggled it with steak knives
in the dark; a ranger
who used it to bait the traps
for bears that bit the tourists; and
a florist in want of oasis,
who pierced it with wired roses.

All along, the brain
was memorizing the names
of crustaceans and flowers, wrestling
with Jacob and the angels, lamenting
the grizzled silver fur. It might have stayed
with the cook forever, fevered
and brothed; but when, on behalf
of the brain, I have called, the cook
hangs up, or doesn't answer.

IV

Encore

I followed a little black dog
past a chalk outline
past a field of blond grasses tipped with frost
a low mauve cloud
a meadow cricket
past Miller's Chicken
past the rain
construction workers in yellow slickers
a river baptism, a little cough,
past the wig-maker's shop & a bald woman
tilting in front of a mirror;
past a flame thrower
& a flame blower
& their pyrotechnics & wedding & the widow
in attendance dancing
under her long black veil—
to a small white house
where a man I didn't recognize stepped out
& clapped me once on the shoulder
& said, Come in, it's been
a disaster without you.

Porch

The diamonds had got in the roses again
I couldn't do anything
couldn't kill myself
couldn't know myself rightly
just sat in that rocker
all summer all day let me
consult no one about this   sorrow
the neighbors came by
with their six-packs and dogs
the webs in the grass went from gold to silver
I needed to mow the lawn

River

On this side, the past—open-faced, broken, butterfly-halved:
Where did they go, the enormous clams, and why

did they leave all these empty white wallets?
Waterbugs stutter the surface and scatter

away from the deep mud-suck of our feet.
Little satellites of trash dislodge and tangle

at our knees. Look at me: fumbling
over the details of her red hair, when

all I meant was to tell you something
about a fish, that hill, or the long blue

blade of dusk which has just begun
to enter the sky, and to punish us.

The Bride Stripped Bare by Her Bachelors, Even

after Duchamp

My satin shines like a milk tooth,
        moonlit ejaculate.
                What elaborate fabric

monster have I become? Swimming
        in crinoline, ballooned.
                I should soon go

swanning in, the glacial
        spectacle, the glad *tableau*
                vivant. I won't go

swooning, heeled, or keel
        my gauzy blowfish dress.
                Which they'd look up!—

as if they'd glimpsed
        aurora borealis (all this silk
                and chandeliering

cannot hide the obvious
        screws.) Am I an obsession?
                I am a machine, a passive

focus. My gown disembarks,
        my gears exposed:
                the feathered motor, leaking.

Licked. Men do not want
        to touch themselves. A quick
                disrobing, & the rub grows

clumsy & derivative. (Seems
   every nude's a bourgeois spoon;
      no polish needed.)

Or I'm untutored, still,
   and the groom's just one more
      empty suitor,

one more formal exercise
   in swallowing
      my mouth.

To My Lover, Returning to His Wife

Because I ignored the rules,
I cannot now myself
cry foul. I do not.

The figs are heavy.

The little house of sticks
which I built for your son
has fallen down in the wind.

Spider Milk

Misspoke, there.

Missed the meeting to distinguish the transient
panhandlers from the homeless.

Missed the bride my best friend jumping
out of her cake.

A rabbit encounters a barbed-wire fence: the figure eight
ensues. The end
result: not undamaged.

A few out of ten thousand silver balloons
make it to the sea.

We detect them in places, deflecting
light, unlike the birds.

What is written appears to be out.

               But you can say it

with diamonds. Forever
flowers.

Conventional Red

When you left,
I took down from the closet
the Grow Your Own Salsa kit
from your mother three Christmases ago.

All week I watched the black soil in its pot—nothing
but white perlite balls and two pillbugs.

This morning, finally, the cotyledons
open, an uproar of green applause.

The sun rolls by on a red leash
dragging a lady
in colossal pink lingerie.

Across the street, the roofers beat
the glittering shingles.

I sit on the stoop and wait
for a few words to find me,
which is not enough to build a good life.

Love Poem

I do not need your whims
or arguments.

You can lie to the moon
about anything, genocide

or magnolias, thumbs
or oranges.

The moon won't even blink.
Don't think

you're immune.
Last week I saw you

in your truck—
you didn't see me—

but we both saw
the man in the astronaut suit

spraying weeds so close
to the beautiful breasts

of the girls' soccer team,
the babies in strollers,

and the about-to-be
flowering cherry.

We drove right by.
I have not changed

the sheets since you left
but I fall asleep

like this: I tell my heart: there
has been no incident.

Coffin Birth (One Theory, Lord)

When we came out   were You already dead?

That might explain the palm trees
where I live—just telephone poles
disguised as palm trees. My best friend's
husband has rosacea. She calls him
Rosie, they laugh and make love
among thirteen pillows on their king-sized
bed. I never had that. The *I want you,*
I mean, *despite your new rash.*

It might also explain all the trash
spinning through the orbit like afterbirth:
the ten-piece Value Meal Buckets,
disposable dog-poop gloves,
and I bet at least one of my bipolar love letters
finally cleared the atmosphere.

Whatever it says, I take it all back.

I have a prescription to keep me
from doing that anymore. I have a prescription
for falling asleep, no late-night sob scrubbing
crusted oats from my wooden spoon.

We are hungry without You, but we are like goats
in the absence of grass.

We finger the scab, but have mostly moved on.

All the Invisible Animals

Past the bridge where wintercress
blooms through the asphalt, and blue

gravel out of nowhere begins a path
through the blond field, you unhook

the leash and tell her, Go on.
She opens her mouth and circles

all the invisible animals—herds
a moth through the yellow weeds,

dreams the little yelp in every shallow
hole and stump.

This is how she satisfies old instincts.
This is how she keeps it

down, the pitiful whine
when you leave in the morning,

the afternoon when you rise
too soon from your stone

and call her back from the river,
at night when across the room

you touch yourself and breathe
into no one's hair, say no one's name.

Those Little Deaths

White toads on the road
so small we didn't even feel them
flatten beneath our shoes.
And mosquitoes—nebulous
clouds we'd clap out, summer
evening's porch talk punctuated,
always, by that strange applause.
Orb-weavers descended at dusk
from their daytime roosts—warm
leaves, the husks of magnolias—
and fastened their threadbare laundry
through the trees. I remember
an enormous spider we smashed,
the difficult flag she'd put up
in our doorframe, the way
she just hung in the middle
and breathed. How soon
we dropped our sticks and turned
to our mother's night-blooming
moonflower; how we cherished
the frantic star it made
against the growing dark.

There Is Also the Suffering of Not Obtaining What Is Desired, Although It Is Sought

Then my teeth hurt.

Then I ate mud, like the earthworm.

Then I saw that dawn back there.

Sometimes John had to tend to a customer,
and Jean had to feed her dogs.

I'd tip back in a kitchen chair,
or set up the game, which wasn't

the point.

     Very early, those stars.

He knew how to go on, a friend had said.

What Constitutes a Proper Planet

I decided to drive to the beach, where I sat in the sand and dug a large hole.
There was a tiny translucent crab with eyes like my mother
and such a specific inner life I tossed it fast back into the tide.
The sop I scooped out made a kind of wall which slid in on itself if my pace slackened.
I had to dig quicker. I dug frantic. Kids appeared with plastic shovels—
I wanted to ask them not to collapse it, but they hung back, a cautious tribe.
Till at last, one poked me with a stick and asked why I was doing that.
And I said, to keep the ocean out. And then they all joined in.

Notes

Page 4: "God Bless Our Crop-Dusted Wedding Cake" is for my father. It is about his life and childhood, not mine.

Page 8: The lines, "You may touch me now, I am tame," and "There's no middle ground, only things and the soul," are variations on lines from John Berryman's *The Dream Songs*, #177 and #385, respectively.

Page 12: "*Bare interior. Grey light. Left/right back: two small windows, curtains drawn,*" adapts the opening scene of Samuel Beckett's *Endgame*.

Page 41: Like all mammals, cows produce milk only to feed their young. In order to satisfy the demands of modern milk production, dairy cows on factory farms must be kept perpetually pregnant, and so are repeatedly artificially inseminated on what some farmers refer to as "the rape rack." The milk intended for their calves is taken several times each day by machines that irritate their sensitive udders, leading to mastitis and infection. Male calves at birth are immediately chained inside veal crates, where they spend sixteen weeks unable to walk or even turn around (the quality of veal requires that no muscle develop) before being slaughtered. Spent dairy cows are subsequently slaughtered for their meat.

Page 46: The epigraph is from *Dream Song #9*, as is the line, "It's golden here in the snow."

Page 58: The title is after Anne Sexton's poem of the same name.

Page 66: The title of this poem is taken from the Dalai Lama's explication of The Four Truths in *The Way to Freedom*: the truth of suffering, the truth of the origin of suffering, the truth of the cessation of suffering, and the truth of the path leading to cessation.